Titian

and Venetian Painting
of the 16th Century

Fundación Amigos del Museo
del Prado
y Alianza Editorial

Floor plan of the Prado Museum

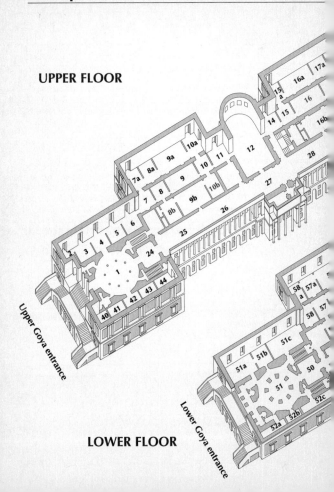

UPPER FLOOR

LOWER FLOOR

Upper Goya entrance

Lower Goya entrance

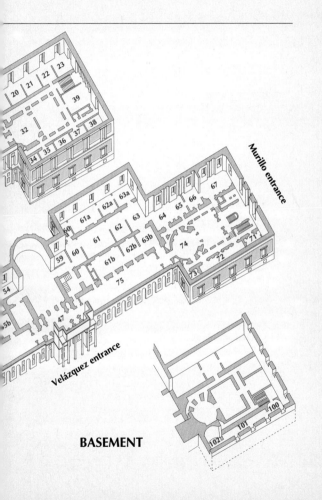

20 21 22 23
39
32
34 35 36 37 38

60
61a 62a 63a
61 62 63
59 60
61b 62b 63b
75

64 65 66 67
63
64
74
72 71
73

Murillo entrance

1
54
55b
47

Velázquez entrance

100
101
102

BASEMENT

Due to the current renovation of the Prado Museum, both the location of the paintings described in this guide and the number of works displayed may vary. We regret any inconvenience this may cause.

Cover and interior design by Ángel Uriarte
Translation by Everett Rice
Axonometric projections by Ana Pazó Espinosa
Layout by Antonio Martín

© Fernando Checa
© Fundación Amigos del Museo del Prado
© Alianza Editorial, S.A., Madrid, 1998
   Calle Juan Ignacio Luca de Tena, 15; 28027 Madrid; teléf.: 393 88 88
   ISBN: 84-206-4287-8
   Depósito legal: M-23137-1997
   Impreso en Altamira, Ctra. de Barcelona, Km 11,200, 28022 Madrid
   Printed in Spain

Introduction

For anyone interested in 16th-century Venetian painting, and in Titian in particular, a visit to the Prado Museum is absolutely necessary. Nowhere else in the world, with the sole exception of Venice itself, can so many of the master's finest paintings be seen in one place. The reason is clear and simple. Titian was the favourite painter of both Charles V and Philip II. And, in the 17th century, Philip IV enlarged the collection of Titian's works, adding others by Veronese, Tintoretto, and Bassano. Thus was formed the largest single collection of 16th-century Venetian painting in Europe. Charles V met Titian in 1530, but their relationship was not cemented until the master's two journeys to Augsburg, in 1547-48 and 1550-51. It was there that he painted some of his best works for the Habsburgs: *La Gloria, Charles V at the Battle of Mühlberg, Philip II in Armour, and* so forth. It was also here that he met Philip II, with whom he collaborated until his death in 1576. This is how the Spanish collection came to have such a large number of works from the painter's final years, which are the ones that reflect our own tastes today. For Philip II, Titian painted not only religious subjects, but portraits, mythology subjects, and allegories, covering the whole range of his production.

Titian's paintings hung in the principal residences of the Habsburgs in Spain, fundamentally in the Royal Alcázar of Madrid and the Monastery of El Escorial. The Alcázar housed most of the mythology subjects, allegories, and portraits. The religious images were kept in El Escorial. In the Alcázar, some of the rooms even took on the names of the paintings they contained. Such was the case of the 'Pieza de las Furias' (Room of the Furies), which for some time held the *Furias* by Titian, and the 'Bóvedas de Tiziano' (Vaulted Rooms of Titian) where Philip IV gathered his prodigious collection of nudes, predominantly the ones by Titian. Whole galleries such as the 'Galería del Mediodía' (South Gallery), which were conceived in the Italian manner and given their definitive arrangement by Velázquez, or state rooms such as the 'Salón de Espejos' (the Hall of Mirrors, which we know today through the paintings of Carreño de Miranda) cannot be comprehended without the absolute presence of Titian and the Venetians of the Renaissance. The Monastery of El Escorial was the second place of importance for the collections of the Venetian School in the times of Philip II and his grandson, Philip IV, who substantially increased the whole collection. The paintings were set out in the ante-sacristy, the sacristy, the chapter rooms, the so-called 'Aula de Moral', and other spaces.

The Alcázar was razed by fire in 1734 and was replaced by the present Royal Palace, where the paintings that were saved from the fire were hung until the first years of the founding of the Prado. The paintings were taken the museum in successive waves in the early 19th century. The disentailment of ecclesiastical properties in the 1830's caused many of the paintings in El Escorial to be moved to the Prado, thus giving rise to the magnificent collection we admire today.

The Venetian school of painting began its development independently within the framework of the Italian Renaissance in the 15th century with artists such as Bellini, Carpaccio, or Antonello da Messina. With Giorgione, the Venetian school joined the advanced modes of the 'Cinquecento'. Giorgione's pupil was Titian, who quickly went beyond his apprenticeship to become one of the great artists of the 16th century. With Titian, the Venetian school reached its zenith. A manner of painting based on 'colorito' became a worthy opposition to the Florentine and Roman idea of painting grounded in intellectualistic 'disegno' and championed by no less a figure than Michelangelo. The two giants, Titian and Michelangelo, embody two of the principal positions of art in the 16th century.

Along with the later stages of Titian's work, the second half of the 16th century witnessed the development of the highly personal styles of Tintoretto and Veronese. They represent two sides of the same coin, which is the Counter-Reformation in Venice: tragic and introspective in Tintoretto, and solemnly majestic in Veronese. This evolution in painting can be followed quite easily in the collection of the Prado Museum.

Giorgione (1478-1510)

The Virgin and Child with Saint Antony of Padua and Saint Roch (Cat. No. 288)

The attribution of this painting is one of the most problematic of all the 16th-century Venetian works in the Prado. The roundness of the forms favour ascribing it to Titian. The calm and static nature of the composition, and above all, the pensive and somewhat daydreamy expression on the faces (especially those of the Virgin and St. Antony) lead us to think this is a Giorgione of the early 16th century, circa 1510. The painting is thought to have been given by the Duke of Medina de las Torres to Philip IV, who placed it in the sacristy of the Monastery of El Escorial.

Lorenzo Lotto (1480-1556)

Micer Marsilio
and his Wife
(Cat. No. 240)

Portrayed are a certain Micer Marsilio and his wife, perhaps members of the Cassotti family of Bergamo. Dated in 1523, this is one of the most pleasant portraits Lotto ever painted. It is a wedding portrait, an unusual facet of this genre in the Renaissance. Inventories made during the second half of the 17th century record this work in the Royal Alcázar of Madrid, hanging in Philip IV's bedroom in the Lower Summer Apartment, where the king died.

Saint Jerome as Penitent
(Cat. No. 448)

Although the first catalogues of the Prado attributed it to Titian, this painting entered El Escorial in 1593 as a work by Lorenzo Lotto. It is one of the best of the many images of the penitent St. Jerome that were destined for this royal monastery. The broad gesture of the protagonist and the whole expression of his body reveal the depth and intimacy of prayer before the image of the Crucifix, which is a fundamental means of quickening pious sentiment.

Sebastiano del Piombo (1485?-1547)

Christ Bearing the Cross (Cat. No. 345)

This painting was probably commissioned in 1520 by the Duke of Sessa, Luis Fernández de Córdoba, Charles V's ambassador to Rome in the 1520's. It did not enter the Spanish royal collections, however, until the 17th century, when Philip IV sent it to the Sacristy of the Monastery of El Escorial. It is one of Sebastiano's most successful prototypes, and very expressive of the pathos which is so characteristic of his religious images.

Sebastiano del Piombo (1485?-1547)

Christ's Descent into Limbo (Cat. No. 346)

From Philip IV's collection at El Escorial, where he placed it in the Sacristy. Painted around 1532. One of Sebastiano's finest compositions in which he shows his taste for pathos and religious emotion. It successfully relies on the grand figure of Christ wrapped in a white shroud, in contrast to the dark tones of the rest of the painting.

Christ Bearing the Cross (Cat. No. 343)

Sebastiano's oft-repeated manner of presenting this subject, of great influence on 16th-century Spanish painting.

Pietà

This painting (c. 1553) comes from the Church of the Saviour in Ubeda. It was a gift from Ferrante Gonzaga to Don Francisco de los Cobos, Charles V's Imperial Secretary, who had it hung in his burial chapel (built according to the plans of Alonso de Vandelvira). The painting now belongs to the Ducal Family of Medinaceli, and is on indefinite loan to the Prado. It is an important work, which shows the special interest this unusual sort of 'Pieta' had for the elite of both Italy and Spain in the 16th century. Sebastiano's figures derive from his highly personal manner of reworking themes taken from Michelangelo. The roundness and monumentality of the figures must surely have commanded the respect of the faithful who went to pray for Don Francisco's soul.

Titian (1485?-1576)

Bacchanal (Cat. No. 418)
Worship of Venus (Cat. No. 419)

These two extraordinary compositions were part of the 'Alabaster Chamber' built for Alfonso I d'Este in Ferrara. He commissioned works from artists like Bellini, Raphael, Fra Bartolomeo, and Titian, although in the end only Bellini and Tit-

ian actually painted anything. These two paintings went from Ferrara to Rome, then to Madrid in 1637, to the great displeasure of the Roman artists of the time, for whom they were a veritable school of painting. In Madrid, they were hung in the 'Bóvedas de Tiziano' in the Alcázar. The iconographical sourse of both paintings can be traced to Philostratus's *Images*, in which he describes a series of paintings from Classical Antiquity.

In the *Worship of Venus*, painted in 1518-1519, a large group of cupids play with the apples they are gathering before a statue of Venus. It is an allegory of love. As Philostratus says: "This is young love and mutual desire. The Erotes playing with the apples are beginning to fall in love... As far as the pair of archers is concerned, they are confirming an already-existing love".

In the *Bacchanal* (1523-1525), we see the effects of wine on the Isle of Andros. A river of wine flows in the foreground as the islanders sing, dance, or sleep under the effects of bacchic delirium.

These two paintings from Titian's youth mark a decisive change in the artist's initial style. We find him abandoning the influence of Bellini and Giorgione on his earlier mythology subjects. They also establish a point of reference for the best artists of the Baroque.

Venus and Music
(Cat. No. 420)
Venus, Love and Music
(Cat. No. 421)

The first of these paintings was done around 1550 and first belonged to Francesco Assonica of Venice, then to Charles I of England, and finally to Philip IV. The history of the second painting is not so certain. It was painted between 1540 and 1550; the first mention of it was not made until it was recorded in the Alcázar of Madrid in 1626. Philip IV had both works installed in the 'Bóvedas de Tiziano' of this royal residence.

Titian (1485?-1576)

They entered the Prado in 1827. Titian painted several versions of this subject, whose meaning can be found in Neoplatonic philosophy: the most immaterial senses (hearing and sight), depicted as a musician who looks on while playing an instrument, are the ones that give us the purest access to beauty, as personified in the nude Venus.

Venus and Adonis
(Cat. No. 422)
Danaë
(Cat. No. 425)

These two canvases are part of the famous series of mythological paintings that Titian himself called *poesie*. They were painted for Philip II between 1553 and 1562. The series was done in pairs. The two paintings in the Prado collection were the first pair that Titian sent to Philip, who was still only a prince. A letter from Titian to Philip while he was in England states this clearly: "And since the Danaë, which I have already sent to Your Majesty (Philip was then king consort to Mary I of England), shows everything from the front I wanted to vary things in this other poem by showing the other side, so that the room where they are displayed will be more pleasing to the eye". He is referring to the *Danaë* and the *Venus* and Adonis. The artist wanted to interest the prince in the formalistic and compositional aspects of the paintings. Each painting shows the opposite view of the female nude. The reclining figure of the *Danaë* is seen from the front, her body extending from left to right, and her right arm closing the composition on the left. The *Venus and Adonis,* however, shows us the goddess's back, with her whole torso and her left arm moving toward the right. This is not only a very clear contrast and opposition of poses, but also a search for contrasts that are complementary. Here, Titian was not trying to create an erotic game. Rather, he was interested in showing how painting could emulate and even surpass sculpture in spite of its unavoidable two-dimensionality. In paint-

ing, it is also possible to contemplate the same figure from several viewpoints. The two stories are based on Ovid's *Metamorphosis.* Danaë has been locked in a tower by her father Acrisius to keep her from conceiving a child. She is visited by Jupiter in the form of a shower of gold. In the other painting, Adonis takes leave of Venus to continue the hunt, where he meets his death. It is possible to make a moral interpretation of these paintings: Danaë reflects impure love based on money, whereas Adonis errs in the moment of refusing the pleasures of the flesh. It is not known where Philip II installed these two *poesie.* Philip IV placed them in the 'Bóvedas de Tiziano' of the Alcázar of Madrid.

Titian (1485?-1576)

Sisyphus (Cat. No. 426)
Tityus (Cat. No. 427)

These are two of the four 'Furies' that Titian painted for Mary of Hungary for her palace in Binche, where they were described by Calvete de la Estrella in 1548. They later entered the collection of Philip II, who installed them in the Alcázar of Madrid, in a room that came to be known as the 'Room of the Furies'. Still later, they adorned the 'Hall of Mirrors' in the same royal residence. They were taken to the Prado in 1828.

Based on classical mythology (one 16th-century traveller to Madrid called them "a Virgilian storm"), they reflect Titian's most clearly Michelangelesque moment. They were seen as allegories on the eternal punishments awaiting rulers of corrupted virtue.

RELIGIOUS SUBJECTS

ATTRIBUTED TO TITIAN
Ecce Homo
(Cat. No. 42)

The attribution of this painting from the El Escorial collections is much-debated. It is a re-working of several motifs from paintings by Titian, such as the *Ecce Homo* (Cat. No. 437).

Salome (Cat. No. 428)

Perhaps from Charles I of England's collection, it went from the Marquess of Leganés's collection to Philip IV's, who placed it in the Alcázar of Madrid. It is a very different version of the melancholy image in the Doria Gallery painted in 1515. Now, at the peak of his career, around 1550, Titian gives us a Salome in motion as she triumphantly displays the head of John the Baptist.

Adam and Eve (Cat. No. 429)

Painted in Titian's maturity, around 1560, this work belonged to Philip II's secretary, Antonio Pérez. It was later confiscated by the King and taken to the Alcázar in Madrid. In the 17th century it was moved from the sacred precincts of the Sacristy to the worldly atmosphere of the so-called 'Bóvedas de Tiziano'. Thus, the idea of the nude in painting prevailed over religious subject matter. A copy by Rubens can also be admired in the Prado.

The Holy Trinity or 'La Gloria' (Cat. No. 432)

This painting was commissioned by Charles V during Titian's second trip to Augsburg in 1551.

The Emperor finally received it in Brussels in Jan uary 1555. He took it to Yuste, and from there it went to El Escorial, where it hung in the 'Aula de Moral' from 1574 to 1839, when it was moved to the Prado.

This is a fundamental painting as far as Titian's relationship with the Austrian-Spanish Habsburgs is concerned. One of the best descriptions of the work comes from Father Santos: "the celebrated 'Gloria' by Titian, in which with the skilful arm of Art, he tends to leave out more than he puts on the canvas. This admirable picture was at San Gerónimo in Yuste, and they brought it hither (to El Escorial) when they brought the body of the Emperor Charles the Fifth, along with all the thronging that Prince occasioned... Our Caesar is portrayed in Glory, with the Empress his wife, and his son, Philip the Second, with many members of the House of Habsburg, who may be recognized in their portraits (being Mary of Hungary and the Princess Juana, and Vargas, the ambassador in Venice, and Titian himself). On the other side are figures from the Old Testament and the New; and in the middle of them all is the Church, depicted as a beautiful Damsel, who seems to be presenting them to the Most Holy Trinity, seated at the top on a Throne of light and majesty, and thereby, the Queen of the Angels: all showing genius, and inventiveness, and lovely poses, very proper movements, excellent colours..."

The Virgin and Child with Saint Dorothy and Saint George (Cat. No. 434)

This painting shows the Virgin Mary and the Christ Child with St. Dorothy and St. George. It is the only work in the Prado from Titian's first period (perhaps around 1515), when Giorgione's influence was still evident. It was acquired by Philip II. Here, Titian's colour is more vivid and harmonious, and the forms are more clearly defined than in his later periods. It was sent to El Escorial in 1593. It entered the Prado in 1839, and was considered to be a Giorgione until the catalogue of 1910.

Christ's Agony in the Garden
(Cat. No. 436)

Titian sent Philip II two paintings on a similar theme. One of them is kept in the Chapter Rooms of the Monastery of El Escorial. This Prado version was sent in 1562 and was formerly in the 'Antesacristía' of El Escorial. This work is a magnificent example of 'night painting', one of Titian's favourite styles. Sadly, the canvas is quite deteriorated today. Father Sigüenza called it "a very courageous painting" since the rather daring night scene is laid out in two very independent spaces. Each space has its own lighting and contrasting sense of scale: in one, the figure of Christ provides the only touch of colour in the entire painting, while in the other, we can only barely make out some figures walking in the foreground, despite their size. We should emphasize the importance of the light from the lantern which one of them is carrying.

Ecce Homo and **Mater Dolorosa**
(Cat. Nᵒˢ. 437, 443, 444)

The first of these three paintings was done by Titian for Charles V in Augsburg in 1548. The Emperor took it with him to the monastery of Yuste when he abdicated. Philip II moved it to El Escorial, where it was paired with the *Mater Dolorosa* or 'Mother of Sorrows' (Cat. No. 444) in 1574. By 1600 both works were in the Alcázar of Madrid, in the 'Oratory of the New Lower Apartment', which indicates that it was moved again in the times of Philip II. The *Ecce Homo* is an important version of a subject Titian painted several times. Here, the artist reflects the idea of resignation in the face of suffering.

The *Mater Dolorosa* (Cat. No. 443), painted in 1554, was also for Charles V. Like the other two, it was taken from Brussels to Yuste and then, in 1571, to El Escorial. Titian was given a model to follow, which clearly shows that the Emperor was interested in securing a specific image for strictly private devotional purposes.

Titian (1485?-1576)

Christ and Simon of Cyrene (Cat. No. 438)

This canvas was acquired by Philip IV and placed in the Alcázar of Madrid. It is quite different from the painting purchased by Philip II (Cat. No. 439), even though both are on the same theme. Painted around 1565, the present painting is more advanced in technique. The protagonists are shown close-up rather than full-length, thus accentuating the work's dramatic meaning.

Christ and Simon of Cyrene (Cat. No. 439)

Painted around 1560, this canvas was sent to El Escorial in 1574. There it was installed in Philip II's private oratory, where it remained until it was moved to the Prado in 1845. Father Sigüenza describes the effects this image had on the King of Spain, when "at night the pious King Philip would remain quite a while meditating on all that he owed the Lord whose shoulders bore such a heavy cross". In this version of the theme, Titian makes use of a subtle interplay of diagonals by counterpointing the hands of Christ with his face and with Simon of Cyrene's hand to enhance the pious meaning of the scene.

Entombment of Christ (Cat. Nos. 440, 441)

Two works of similar composition but different treatment of colour. The first (the one of higher quality) was painted in 1559. It is a decisive work from the beginning of Titian's final period. The conception of the scene differs radically from the more classical version now in the Louvre. It arrived at El Escorial in 1574 and was placed on the Epistle side of the 'Old Church', next to two other important Titians which are still *in situ:* the *Martyrdom of St. Lawrence* and the *Adoration of the Magi.* The second of the Prado's two paintings is from the 1570's. In the opinion of some specialists, it is a product of Titian's workshop. It may have come from the collection of Philip II's secretary, Antonio Pérez.

Christ as a Gardener
(Cat. No. 442)

This is a fragment of a painting from 1553 that belonged to Mary of Hungary (Charles V's sister and a great lover of the arts). We know the general appearance of the larger original through a copy by Alonso Sánchez Coello in El Escorial. Acquired by Philip II and sent to El Escorial in 1574.

Saint Margaret
(Cat. No. 445)

This painting, dated in 1565, could be found, at least in the 17th century, in the Church of San Jerónimo el Real in Madrid. From there it was taken to the Royal Alcázar and hung in its 'Galería del Mediodía'. Antonio Palomino described it there, although the painting he mentions could well have been another version of the same subject. Titian painted another, very similar version of the same subject for the young Prince Philip, which is the one now exhib-

Counter-Reformation concern for images in the struggle against evil. Evil is symbolized here by the monster in the lower part of the canvas that contrasts greatly with the magnificent figure of the saint in contraposto. In the background, we see a phantasmagoric and highly suggestive image of the city of Venice.

ited in El Escorial. In spite of the problems that arose from the nakedness of the leg ("they added false clothing", says Father Sigüenza, "to cover a nude leg, which was a gross consideration"). Even so, this painting is a good example of

Saint Margaret
(Cat. No. 446)

This painting by Titian's workshop has sometimes been attributed to Palma Giovane. It may have been purchased by Philip II for El Escorial, but the first sure mention of it was not until the 17th century. Its inferior quality leads us to attribute it to the master's workshop.

Titian (1485?-1576)

PORTRAITS

Self-Portrait
(Cat. No. 407)

Purchased by Philip IV at the sale of Rubens's estate and placed in the Alcázar of Madrid. It entered the Prado in 1821. It is the poignant last self-portrait of the artist, as an old man dressed in black. Only his very intense face, the golden chain (a sign of his nobility), and his hand holding a brush stand out, in clear self-celebration of his profession. This also alludes to the liberality of the art of painting. It can be dated between 1565 and 1570.

Federigo Gonzaga, Duke of Mantua (Cat. No. 408)

Son of Isabella d'Este, one of the most famous art collectors in the Renaissance, Federigo Gonzaga was raised to the rank of duke by Charles V in 1530. He was also one of Titian's greatest patrons and presented him to the Emperor. This painting went from Mantua to England (to Charles I's

collection) and from there to the Marquess of Leganés, whose heirs gave it to Philip IV. Philip IV placed it in the 'Galería del Mediodía' of the Alcázar of Madrid. It entered the Prado in 1821. Probably painted in 1523, this is one of the best portraits from Titian's youthful maturity. It is very expressive of the arrogance and majesty with which the Italian aristocracy liked to be portrayed during the Renaissance.

Charles V (Cat. No. 409)

This is the only surviving example of the first po-traits Titian made of Charles V. It was painted in Bologna in 1533. Perhaps at the Emperor's own wish, the artist copied a similar work by the German artist Jacob Seisenegger (Kunsthistorisches Museum, Vienna), an unusual fact that still has no satisfactory explanation. This is one of the artist's best portraits, and was of fundamental importance in the development of State portraiture. In 1623, it was given by Philip IV to the Prince of

Wales (the future King Charles I of England). Later, Philip IV bought it back in the sale of Charles's estate after his execution. It entered the Prado in 1821.

Charles V at the Battle of Mühlberg (Cat. No. 410)

This famous painting establishes the core of the Habsburgs' patronage of Titian. It was painted in Augsburg in 1548, immediately after Charles's victory over the Protestant princes of the League of Smalkalda. From Mary of Hungary's collection it went to Philip II, who installed it in the Alcázar of Madrid. During the reign of Philip IV it was placed in the Alcázar's room of honour, called the 'Salón Nuevo' or 'Salón de Espejos'. It entered the Prado in 1827. The painting marks the beginning of the genre of equestrian portraiture, whose subsequent success influenced artists such as Rubens and Velázquez. It depicts Charles V on horseback, with the weapons he used on the day of the Battle of Mühlberg Despite its apparent simplicity, this work is highly symbolic: the equestrian image of Charles V alludes to the Roman emperors, primarily to Marcus Aurelius, whose equestrian portrait still exists in Rome. It also refers to the imagery of the 'Soldier of Christ' in Renaissance humanism, and to Erasmus, in particular (which i8 why it has been associated with Durer's famous engraving, *Knight, Death and the Devil*). Charles's expressionless face alludes to the idea of the Emperor's self-possession and self-control, in the manner of Marcus Aurelius's beloved doctrine of stoicism. The painting also refers to Charles as a new, Christian Hercules who overcomes his enemies and, then, himself. Finally, the twilight alludes to Joshua's battle against the Amalekites, when, by divine command, the Sun stood still. The Elbe River in the background refers to the Rubicon of Julius Caesar...

But, above all, Titian has accomplished a deep and purely visual reflection on the person of Charles and his cultural environment. This is one of the finest examples of

itian's insight into history, in
which the complex world of
symbolism is not painted
directly, but merely alluded

to, thus making this one of the
most subtle artistic achievements in the whole history of
painting.

Titian (1485?-1576)

Philip II
(Cat. No. 411)

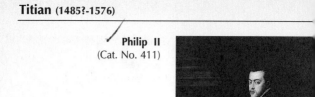

This portrait was painted in Augsburg, on Titian's second trip there, when the young Philip was ending his first journey in Europe between 1548 and 1551. Philip's first reaction upon seeing it was a curious one: in a letter sent to his aunt, Mary of Hungary, he said he thought it had been painted too hastily. The future king of Spain, brought up on the Flemish school's taste for minute detail, could not yet understand Titian's painterly technique at its height.

This is a fundamental work in the development of the so-called 'State portrait', with the personage depicted full-length and life-sized, with one hand on his sword and the other resting on the table next to his helmet. By the end of Philip II's reign, it was mentioned as being in the 'Guarda joyas' or treasure-room of the Alcázar. From there, in the 17th century, it went to the 'Galería del Mediodía' of the same Alcázar. It entered the Prado in 1827.

Gentleman with a Clock
(Cat. No. 412)

This gentleman has never been identified. The painting entered the royal collections during the reign of Philip IV, perhaps as a gift from Niccolò Ludovisi. It hung in the stairwell of the royal guards' room in the Alcázar of Madrid. A late work, from around 1550.

Daniele Barbaro
(Cat. No. 414)

ırbaro was one of the most nportant intellectuals in ¿nice in the l6th century. He anslated and commented on Vitruvius's treatise on chitecture, which was ccompanied by illustrations / Andrea Palladio. In 1567, e wrote his *Prattica della* *Prospettiva*. Painted in 1545, this portrait had been in the Spanish royal collections since the 17th century, hanging in the Alcázar of Madrid.

Titian (1485?-1576)

Empress Isabella (Cat. No. 415)

Isabella (1503-1539) was the daughter of King Manuel I of Portugal and his wife María, who was the daughter of Ferdinand and Isabella. She married Charles V in Seville in 1526 and became Philip II's mother in 1527. Even though Titian never saw her, he painted her portrait at least three times, always following earlier models. This work is notable for the sumptuousness of the clothing, the magnificence of the landscape, and the perhaps intentionally expressionless face. The portrait was painted in Augsburg in 1548 at Charles V's command. The Emperor took it with him when he retired to the Monastery of Yuste. It was moved to the Alcázar of Madrid by Philip II, and entered the Prado in 1821.

HISTORY AND ALLEGORY

Marqués del Vasto Adressing his Troops (Cat. No. 417)

The Marqués del Vasto, Alfonso de Ávalos (1502-1546), was one of the most important Italian military men in Charles V's service. The painting, dated between 1539 and 1541, may allude to an incident in the campaign against the Turks in Hungary in 1539, which allowed Titian to praise the marquess as a Classical hero, since his posture is akin to some of the Roman generals on Trajan's Column as well as the *Allocution of Constantine* by Giulio Romano in the Vatican. From Charles I's collection, it later belonged to Philip IV, who placed it in the Alcázar of Madrid. It entered the Prado in 1828.

Spain Comes to the Aid of Religion (Cat. No. 430)

In 1566, this painting was a mythology scene with the figures of Minerva and Neptune. After the Battle of Lepanto (1571), in order to add it to the collections of Philip II, the original allegory was transformed into an allegory of Spain, and Neptune's chariot turned into one ridden by a Turk. Thus changed, it was sent to Madrid in 1575 and placed in the Oratory of the Alcázar. It was sent to El Escorial in the 17th century and entered the Prado i 1839.

Philip II Offering Prince Ferdinand to God
(Cat. No. 431)

This painting was commissioned by Philip II in 1573 to commemorate two events that the king considered to be of utmost importance: the birth of a new heir, Prince Ferdinand (who died in 1578), and the victory at Lepanto in the same year. Philip II placed it in the Alcázar, and Philip IV installed it in the 'Salón de los Espejos'. It entered the Prado in 1839. The painter Alonso Sánchez Coello may have sent the composition to Titian.

It was later enlarged by Vicente Carducho to adapt it to the frames of the 'Salón de los Espejos'. Although the presence of Titian's helpers has been pointed out, the work has some splendid passages, such as the foreshortening of the angel and, above all, the battle of Lepanto, whose sudden blazes, mixed with air, clouds, and water inspired Velázquez for his buffoon *Don Juan de Austria* (also in the Prado).

Bernardo Licinio (1489-1560)

Agnese, the Painter's Sister-in-Law (Cat. No. 289) An excellent family portrait. The painter was born in Poscante de Bergamo in 1489 and died in Venice in 1560. From the royal collections.

Lambert Sustris (c. 1515-1599)

Baptism of Christ (Cat. No. 581) Sustris was a Flemish artist who lived in Venice in the 16th century. As this painting shows, he skilfully adapted himself to Titian's style. His principal work, *Charles V Seated* (Alte Pinakothek, Munich) was long considered to be by Titian.

Antonio Badile (1517-1560)

Unknown Lady (Cat. No. 485) It was Berensen who attributed this painting to Badile, while others still ascribe it to the school of Veronese. It is a portrait in the Venetian manner without greater pretensions. It comes from the royal collections.

Jacopo Tintoretto (1518?-1594)

Bible Stories (Cat. Nos. 394, 395, 386, 396, 388, 389)

These works are among the best examples of Tintoretto's so-called 'Veronesian' period. It was a youthful moment, around 1555, in which we clearly see Veronese's influence in terms of colour, rich garments, and the importance given to architecture. Some specialists have spoken of a taste for narrative which developed in a decorative manner as the product of an exquisitely mannerist sensibility.

The paintings must have been purchased by Velázquez in Venice, and in Madrid they decorated the alcove of the first room of the 'Bovedas de Tiziano'. They were placed around another Tintoretto in the Prado collection which i. not on display: *The Purifica tion of the Plunder of the Mid ianite Virgins*. This ceiling arrangement, as it must have been in Venice, explains the forced look of the architecture in the paintings, which were made to be seen almost vertically from below. The pompous and exaggerated colour and the sensuality of the series determined the non-religious use of them in Philip IV's collection, despite their religious subject matter. The themes depicted are: *Solomon and the Queen of Sheba, The Finding of Moses,*

Susanna and the Elders, Esther and Ahasuerus, Joseph and Potiphar's Wife, and Judith and Holofernes.

Judith and Holofernes (Cat. No. 391)

This painting once belonged to the Marqués de la Ensenada, and entered the royal collections in the 17th century. A recent cleaning has uncovered an excellent Tintoretto with colder colour. The postures and the composition are thoroughly Mannerist.

Jacopo Tintoretto (1518?-1594)

Baptism of Christ
(Cat. No. 397)

This painting is related to others of the same subject in the Church of San Silvestro in Venice and the Cleveland Museum of Art. It is highly expressive of Tintoretto's maturity, and can be dated around 1580. It was mentioned in the royal collections in the early 19th century.

Paradise
(Cat. No. 398)

This is not, as has often been thought, a model for Tintoretto's famous work in the Doges' Palace in Venice. The differences are many. It is most likely a replica that the artist made for a private client. It was later purchased by Velázquez for the Alcázar of Madrid. It is a good example of Tintoretto's ability for large compositions. What stands out here is his overall vision and his Mannerist approach to arrangements, colour, and posture in the mass of figures in the painting.

Christ Washing the Apostles' Feet
(Cat. No. 2824)

Purchased by Philip IV in the sale of the estate of Charles I of England, this painting was installed in the Sacristy of El Escorial, where it is described in many sources until its move to the Prado in 1940. Painted between 1547-1548, it is the Prado's finest Tintoretto. The best description of it comes from Father Santos: "The great Tintoretto outdid himself here. Its inventiveness and execution are of most excellent fancy. Anyone who sees it can only with difficulty be persuaded that it is painted and not real, such is the strength of its colours, and the arrangement in perspective. It seems

hat one could enter the pic-
ure, and walk across the floor
paved with multi-coloured
tiles which get smaller and
smaller, making the distance
in the room seem greater, and
the space between the figures
quite airy... The Disciples are
preparing themselves for the
washing-of-feet, looking on
in confusion at such a strange
example of humility being set
by their Master... The Table
in the middle, the seats, and
the dog lying on the floor are
real, not painted. Let us say
once and for all: no matter
how many paintings were put
alongside this canvas, they
would all still be paintings,
and only make this one all the
more real."

PORTRAITS

Sebastiano Veniero
(Cat. No. 366)

Until 1951, it was thought to
portray Sebastiano Veniero,
but the inscription that sup-
ported this hypothesis was
removed at that time because
it was a later addition. It
comes from the royal collections, though its identification
in the inventories is difficult.
It could be dated between
1570 and 1580.

Jacopo Tintoretto (1518?-1594)

Archbishop Peter
(Cat. No. 369)

The Prado catalogue questions whether this may be a portrait of Peter of Bourbon, Archbishop of Pisa. It came from Isabella Farnese's collection at the Palace of La Granja.

A Jesuit
(Cat. No. 370)

The identity of the sitter is not known. Its attribution to Tintoretto is unsure. Even though Berenson thought it was a late work, it has recently been attributed to Domenico Tintoretto. In the Alcázar of Madrid in the 17th century.

A Senator
(Cat. No. 371)

It was formerly attributed to Titian, although today it is thought to be a Tintoretto. From the royal collections.

Venetian Magistrate
(Cat. No. 373)

The attribution of this work, which came from the royal collections, is questioned. It has recently been ascribed to Domenico Tintoretto, Jacopo's son.

Venetian Magistrate
(Cat. No. 374)

His clothing indicates his rank in the city government. This type of official portrait was much cultivated by Tintoretto.

Jacopo Tintoretto (1518?-1594)

Venetian Patrician
(Cat. No. 377)

It comes from the royal collections, although it has not been located in the inventories. It is considered to be one of Tintoretto's first experiences in the field of portraiture. Probably between 1546-1548.

**Gentleman
with a Golden Chain**
(Cat. No. 378)

Painted in the 1560's, this is not only one of Tintoretto's finest portraits at the Prado, but also one of the best of his whole career. It was installed in the 'Galería del Mediodía' in the Alcázar of Madrid. It is very expressive of Tintoretto's concept of portraiture. The austere sitter is painted practically in monochrome. His imposing presence is not only physical and sensual, as in so many works by Veronese or Titian; it is also fundamentally moral.

Jacopo Tintoretto (1518?-1594)

Senator
(Cat. No. 379)

This may be a portrait of Marco Grimaldi. Other portraits of him can be found in London and Vienna. It comes from the royal collections and is a typical example of a genre Tintoretto knew well: portraits of Venetian political figures.

Young Venetian Woman
(Cat. No. 382)
La Tintoretta
(Cat. No. 384)
Portrait
(Cat. No. 385)

The inventories of the Alcázar of Madrid often mention portraits of Venetian women attributed to Tintoretto. They may refer to the series at the Prado, three of which are on view. Some of them have been ascribed to Jacopo's daughter, 'La Tintoretta', though not the three now on display. Of them all, the best is No. 382, one of the most attractive images Tintoretto ever painted. Its magnificent interplay of greys, whites, and purples is extraordinarily subtle and refined. It is at once cold and sensual, and like the rest of the series, it must be under- stood in the context of the very specific kind of Venet- ian portraiture, of courtesans. These paintings may be the "Eight portrait heads on eight canvases" that hung in the 'Galería del Mediodía' of the Alcázar of Madrid in the 17th century.

HISTORY SUBJECT

Battle between Turks and Christians (Cat. No. 399)

Today, we know that the theme of this work is the 'Abduction of Helen'. Although this is explicit in the lower left corner, it is con- cealed in the typically Man- nerist confusion of the com- position, and in the equally characteristic use of cold colour. Painted between 1580 and 1585, it may have been purchased by Velázquez for the 'Hall of Mirrors' in the Alcázar of Madrid.

Giovanni Battista Moroni (1523-1578)

A Soldier
(Cat. No. 262)

Moroni was a painter from the northern Italian region of Bergamo (where he died in 1578). He specialized in portraits which at times used the full-length format. This is not the case of the Prado painting, which hung in the Alcázar of Madrid in the 17th century.

Paolo Veronese (1528?-1588)

Venus and Adonis (Cat. No. 482)

This painting was purchased by Velázquez in Venice and installed in the 'Galería del Mediodía' of the Alcázar of Madrid. It is one of the artist's absolute masterpieces. Following Ovid's *Metamorphosis,* it shows Adonis sleeping on Venus's lap just before he goes off on a hunt and is ripped to pieces by a wild boar.

Paolo Veronese (1528?-1588)

Ovid narrates the laziness and sensuality of the moment and delights in describing the coolness of the grass in the shade of the tree. Veronese has followed this literary idea: he places the couple in an opulent atmosphere of green fields and trees. The play of light and shadow on the body of the naked Venus is truly prodigious, as is the indolence of the sleeping Adonis. The interplay of colour, in the contrasting oranges, golds, and a wide range of greens, is one of the greatest achievements of Veronese's entire career.

RELIGIOUS SUBJECTS

Susanna and the Elders (Cat. No. 483)

This painting comes from Veronese's final period, around 1580. Most noteworthy is the setting where the action takes place: a typically Mannerist Venetian-style garden with an architectural fasade of clearly Palladian origin. The canvas was first cited in the inventories of the Alcázar of Madrid in the 17th century.

The Virgin and Child with Saint Lucy and a Martyr
(Cat. No. 490)

This is a typical work of pious iconography in the Venetian manner, with the figures shown half-length. In contrast to paintings of this kind from the first half of the 16th century, here the artist has introduced greater action and movement, as is common in these later years. It is attributed, with some doubts, to Paolo Veronese. From the collections of the Alcázar of Madrid.

Dispute with the Doctors in the Temple (Cat. No. 491)

The Venetian chronicler Ridolfi described this painting in 1648 as existing in the house of the Contarini family of Padua. It may have been purchased by Velázquez in Italy. It was hung in a place of honour in the 'Hall of Mirrors' of the Alcázar of Madrid. It is a splendid work from Veronese's maturity. It is dated 1548 on the edge of the book. The painter has created a theatrical setting by means of

Paolo Veronese (1528?-1588)

classical architecture in the Payladian manner, and in his wise positioning of the figures. He places the figures in a circle around Christ, and the whole arrangement is majestically emphasized by the colonnade and the background architecture. This theatrical convergence towards a focal point is further accentuated by the attitudes of the figures themselves. The man standing in the centre with his back to the viewer, the gesture of the one sitting on the right, and the looks on their faces, also carry us towards the centre of the work.

Jesus and the Centurion (Cat. No. 492)

This is one of Veronese's best paintings in the Prado. It was probably painted between 1570 and 1575. Ridolfi described it in 1648 in the Contarini house of Padua. Later, it was purchased for Philip IV at the sale of Charles I of England's estate upon his execution. It was later hung in the Chapter Rooms of El Escorial.

Very close in style to the magnificent *Darius before Alexander* at London's National Gallery, the composition is resolved in the manner of a frieze. The play of gestures in the two groups and the counterposition of the two protagonists lend a sense of contained drama to the scene. Veronese's custom of dressing the protagonists in the luxurious garments of the day gives the painting an air of richness. The classical architecture reinforces the sensation of a 'live performance'. Also worth noting is how the balustrade and the wall in the background become a 'frons scenae' because they are lighted in a different manner and shown in different perspective.

Marriage at Cana
(Cat. No. 494)

This work was acquired by Philip IV at the sale of Charles I of England's estate upon his execution. It was placed in the Chapter Rooms of El Escorial. It may well be a product of Veronese's workshop.

49

Paolo Veronese (1528?-1588)

Martyrdom of Saint Mennas
(Cat. No. 497)

This painting, dated around 1580, was given to Philip IV by Alfonso Enríquez de Cabrera, Admiral of Castile. It was hung in the 'Aula de Moral' in El Escorial. It entered the Prado in 1837. There is a replica of it in the Cerralbo Museum of Madrid. Although there may have been participation by members of his workshop, it is a good example of Veronese's treatment of the theme of martyrdom. He places the saint and the executioner in a group which is to be seen from below. He emphasizes this perspective by means of the classical architecture in the background.

Mary Magdalene as Penitent
(Cat. No. 498)

This is an eloquent example of the expressive possibilities that Veronese had from a religious point of view. The painting, dated 1583, entered the royal collections in the times of Isabella Farnese and was kept at the Palace of La Granja.

Youth between Vice and Virtue
(Cat. No. 499)

This clearly moralizing work is from Veronese's final years, around 1580. It is mentioned in the inventories of the Alcázar of Madrid during the 17th century.

Noteworthy is the grouping of the youth with Virtue and the classical architecture in the background, which is quite typical of Veronese's work.

✓ **Sacrifice of Isaac**
(Cat. No. 500)

In 1837 this painting was taken to the Prado from the Sacristy of El Escorial, where it had been since the 17th century. It is a good example of Veronese's ability to play with foreshortening, as in the figure of the angel, with forced postures (Abraham), and with soft tonalities.

Paolo Veronese (1528?-1588)

Family of Cain
(Cat. No. 501)

Painted around 1580, this is one of the most interesting of the artist's last works. In the context of Veronese's opulent and theatrical art, this painting is remarkable for its unusual economy of means. Also worth noting are the dark tones of the colour in general, and the simple landscape on the right. It is recorded in the so-called 'Pieza Oscura' (Dark Room) of the Alcázar in the second half of the 17th century.

The Finding of Moses
(Cat. No. 502)

This is one of Veronese's best works in the Prado. It comes from the royal collections, where it is recorded as having hung in various places in the Alcázar of Madrid.

More than the grandioseness, majesty, and theatricality found in many of Veronese's other works, what stands out here is his great capacity for refinement and delicacy, which reminds us of Tiepolo and the Rococo. The composition is very wisely structured. The figures in the principal scene form an arc centred on the figure of Moses and the lady who observes the child. Moses is flanked by two touches of red from the black man on the left and the dwarf on the right. The group is set against a background composed of a city, a landscape, and the softly-nuanced hues of a blue sky. Almost a miniature, this painting is an extraordinary example of Veronese's ability to work on an intimate scale, even though he was an artist who specialized in large formats.

Paolo Veronese (1528?-1588)

Livia Colonna
(Cat. No. 486)

This may not be a portrait of Livia Colonna, who was murdered in 1552, unless it was done 'in memoriam'. Today, it is thought to have been purchased by Philip IV from the sale of Rubens's estate and hung in the Alcázar of Madrid. It is a magnificent colouristic portrait from Veronese's final years, perhaps painted between 1570-1580. It shows the chromatic opulence and sensuality so characteristic of the artist's work.

Lavinia Vecellio
(Cat. No. 487)

Titian painted several portraits of his daughter, Lavinia, who was born before August 1530. This work comes from the royal collections, and was listed at the Buen Retiro Palace in Madrid at the end of the 18th century.

Carleto Veronese (1579-1596)

Saint Agatha
(Cat. No. 480)

This work by Veronese's son, which is rather routine in its execution, was sent to El Escorial in 1593 by Philip II and was installed in the infirmary cloister.

Jacopo Bassano (1510/15-1592)

RELIGIOUS SUBJECTS

Adam Warned (Cat. No. 21) **Noah's Ark** (Cat. No. 22)

Executed around 1569, these two works wre acquired by Philip IV from Emmanuele Filiberto of Savoy. The king hung them in one of his bedrooms in the Alcázar of Madrid. They are two excelent examples of the artist's interest in minute, naturalistic detail in painting animals, one of his most characteristic traits.

Jacopo Bassano (1510/15-1592)

Adoration of the Shepherds
(Cat. Nos. 25-26)

These two paintings come from the royal collections. They show one of the more noteworthy aspects of the Bassano family's production: 'night paintings'. This genre was successful in Venice and the North of Italy. It was decisive in the subsequent evolution of painting in the early 17th century.

Christ Cleansing the Temple
(Cat. No. 27)
Moses Drawing Water from the Rock
(Cat. No. 6312)

These paintings, done between 1563 and 1564, are two equally typical scenes showing the artist's taste for a certain anecdotal and naturalistic complexity in his religious and Biblical paintings. The bearded man on the left in the *Cleansing of the Temple* who is hastily picking up his money from a table is Titian. Both are from the royal collections.

Jacopo Bassano (1510/15-1592)

Self-Portrait (Cat. No. 32)   A painter's son himself, Jacopo was born in Bassano del Grappa in 1510, where he died in 1592. He was the most important member of a family totally dedicated to painting. By the end of the 16th century, their workshop was highly successful, both in Venice and its environs and throughout Europe. This is attested by the abundance of copies, replicas, and repetitions of similar themes.

Leandro Bassano (1557-1622)

RELIGIOUS SUBJECTS

Crowning with Thorns
(Cat. No. 41)   This painting was once part of the royal collections. It can be classified within the genre of 'night painting'.

PORTRAITS

Magistrate or Priest
(Cat. No. 45)   This work from the royal collections shows the influence of Pasarotti.

Anonymous Italian

Mystic Marriage of Saint Catherine
(Cat. No. 270)

This painting entered the Spanish royal collections in the times of Isabella Farnese and was hung in the Palace of La Granja. It has been attributed to Palma Giovane, Lambert Sustris, and Domenico Tintoretto. In any case, its iconography is often found in Italian Renaissance painting. Its composition, with half-length figures, is quite typical of 16th century Venetian art.

Other paintings of the Venetian School outside the Prado Museum

The enormous production of Titian, Tintoretto, Veronese, and the Bassani throughout the 16th century has made it possible to find their paintings in an infinite number of museums all over the world. We shall limit ourselves here to pointing out some of the most important works that come from the Spanish royal collections (the nucleus of the Prado) but which are to be found outside the Museum's walls. To this we shall add a very brief selection of these masters' works in Venice itself. The first obligatory visit is, of course, to El Escorial, where we can admire masterpieces by Titian such as the *Martyrdom of St. Lawrence* (in the 'Old Church'), *St. Jerome* and the *Agony in the Garden* (Chapter Rooms), and the *Crucifixion* (Sacristy). Here too can be found several Bassanos, and two paintings by Tintoretto and Veronese (with considerable participation of their workshops) which were originally meant for the main altarpiece of the Basilica: the *Adoration of the Shepherds* and the *Annunciation.* From the collection of Philip IV, we should highlight a a *Christ in the Sepulchre* by Domenico Tintoretto, a *Descent into Limbo* by Veronese, and two Tintorettos: *Christ and Mary Magdalene* and *Esther and Ahasuerus.*

The rest of Titian's *poesies* for Philip II can be seen in the National Gallery of Edinburgh *(Diana and Callisto, Diana and Actaeon);* the Wallace Collection *(Perseus and Andromeda)* and the National Gallery *(Death of Actaeon)* in London; and the Isabella Stewart Gardner Museum of Boston *(Rape of Europe).* The National Gallery of London also has *The Tribute to Caesar,* from Philip II's collection, and a *Virgin and Child* from Philip Philip IV's. The Alte Pinakothek in Munich has Titian's superb *Virgin and Child,* which belonged to Philip II. The Fitzwilliam Museum in Cambridge has Titian's magnificent *Tarquin and Lucretia,* painted for the same monarch. The Louvre in Paris has the *Jupiter and Antiope* and the famous *Venus del Pardo* by Titian. And, finally, we should indicate the existence of a *Cephalus and Procris* by Veronese which was paired with his *Venus and Adonis,* now in the Museum of Fine Arts in Strasbourg.

Most of these paintings left Spain at the time of the French invasion in the 19th century, or immediately afterwards, as 'gifts' to French generals. The notable exception would be Titian's poesies, which Philip V gave to the Duke of Grammont in 1704 as a token of his appreciation for the Duke's behaviour during the War of the Spanish Succession.

In Venice, aside from the Gallery of the Academy, the most interesting attractions are the works that are still *in situ.* The most important places are the Doge's Palace, the Church and School of San Rocco; the Madonna dell'Orto (Tintoretto), the Churches of I Frari (Titian), La Salute (Titian), Jesuits (Titian, Tintoretto), San Salvatore (Titian), San Sebastiano (Veronese), San Giorgio Maggiore (Tintoretto), San Marcuola (Tintoretto), and many more.

The Thyssen-Bornemisza Museum in Madrid has some excellent Titians, such as the *St. Jerome* and a portrait of the *Doge Alessandro Venier,* a few Tintorettos such as *Paradise,* and the magnificent portrait of *Ferry Carondolet and his Secretaries* by Sebastiano del Piombo. In the same collection are Lorenzo Lotto's *Self-Portrait,* Palma Vecchio's *La Bella,* and Jacopo Bassano's *Parable of the Sower.*

Basic Chronology

Circa 1477: Birth of Giorgione in Castelfranco del Veneto.

Circa 1480: Birth of Lorenzo Lotto in Venice.

1485: Birth of Sebastiano del Piombo in Venice.

Circa 1488: Birth of Titian in Piave di Cadore.

1500: Birth of Charles V in Ghent.

1505: Birth in Brussels of Mary of Hungary, Charles V's sister and collector of Titians.

Circa 1510: Birth of Jacopo Bassano in Bassano del Grappa. By this time, Giorgione is already dead.

1515: Titian, *Sacred and Profane Love* (Rome, Borghese Gallery).

1516-1518: Titian paints the *Assumption* for the Frari Church in Venice.

1517: Alfonso d'Este decides to use mythology paintings to decorate the Alabaster Chamber in Ferrara. Titian paints the *Bacchanal* and the *Worship of Venus* for this room.

1519: *Madonna di Ca'Pesaro* by Titian at I Frari in Venice.

1519: Birth of Tintoretto in Venice.

1527: Birth of Philip II in Valladolid.

1528: Birth of Veronese in Venice.

1530: First contact between Titian and Charles V.

1533: Titian is knighted by Charles V.

1536: Tintoretto begins to work as an independent master in Venice.

1536-1538: Titian's series of 'The Emperors' for Federigo Gonzaga in Mantua. Later in Philip IV's possession. Destroyed in the Alcázar fire in 1734.

1548: Death of Sebastiano del Piombo.

1548-1551: Philip II's first trip to the Low Countries. First contact with Titian.

1548: *Miracle of St. Mark* by Tintoretto (Academy Gallery, Venice).

1548: The Battle of Mühlberg. Charles V defeats Protestants of the Smalkalda League.

1548: Titian's first trip to Augsburg, at Charles V's request.

1551: Titian's second trip to Augsburg, at Charles V's request.

1554-1559: Philip II's second trip to the Low Countries.

1555: Veronese moves definitively to Venice.

1557: Death of Lorenzo Lotto.

1558: Death of Charles V in Yuste and Mary of Hungary in Cigales (Valladolid).

1563: Work starts on El Escorial.

1564: Tintoretto begins the paintings of the 'Sala del Albergo' in the Scuola di San Rocco in Venice. Finished in 1566.

1573: Veronese paints the *Marriage at Cana* (Louvre) for San Giorgio Maggiore in Venice.

1574: Philip II installs a great number of Titians in El Escorial.

1575: Tintoretto begins the paintings for the 'Sala Grande' of the Scuola di San Rocco in Venice. Finished in 1578.

1576: Death of Titian in Venice.

1577: Last fire at the Doges' Palace in Venice. Start of its redecoration (as it remains to this day).

1583: Veronese paints *Triumph of Venice* for the Doges' Palace.

1583-1587: Paintings of Tintoretto for the 'Lower Room' of the Scuola di San Rocco.

1588: Veronese dies in Venice.

1592: Death of Jacopo Bassano in Bassano del Grappa.

1593: Philip II sends several important Titians to El Escorial.

1594: Death of Tintoretto in Venice.

1598: Death of Philip II in El Escorial.

1599: Birth of Velázquez in Seville.

1621: Philip IV accedes to the throne of Spain.

1648-1651: Velázquez's second trip to Italy, where he buys important Venetian paintings for Philip IV.

1652: Velázquez is appointed Chamberlain. He begins to take charge of the royal art collection, with special attention to the Alcázar of Madrid and the Monastery of El Escorial.

1660: Death of Velázquez.

1666: Death of Philip IV.

1734: Fire at the Alcázar of Madrid, in which many paintings of the Venetian school are destroyed.

Basic Bibliography

ARSLAN, W.: *I Bassano,* Milan, 1960.

BERENSON, B.: *The Venetian Painters of the Renaissance,* New York-London, 1894.

Beroqui, P.: *Tiziano en el Museo del Prado,* Madrid, 1946.

Catalogue: *The Genius of Venice, 1500-1600,* London, 1983.

Catalogue: *Jacopo Bassano c. 1510-1592,* Bologna, 1992.

Catalogue: *El Real Alcázar de Madrid. Dos siglos de architectura y coleccionismo en la corte de los Reyes de España,* Madrid, 1993.

Catalogue: *Le siècle de Titien,* Paris, 1993.

Catalogue: *Tiziano,* Venice, 1990.

Catalogue: *Tintoretto, I ritratti,* Venice, 1994.

CROWE, J. A. - CAVALCASELLE, G. B.: *Tiziano, la sua vita e i suoi tempi,* Florence, 1877-1878.

CHECA, F.: *Felipe II, mecenas de las artes,* Madrid, 1992.

CHECA, F.: *Tiziano y la monarquía hispánica,* Madrid, 1994.

FEHL, P. P.: *Decorum and Wit. The Poetry of Venetian Painting,* Vienna, 1992.

HOPE, C.: *Titian,* London, i980.

HIRST, M.: *Sebastiano del Piombo,* Oxford, 1981.

HUMFREY, P.: *Painting in Renaissance Venice,* New Haven-London, 1995.

PALLUCHINI, P.: *Paolo Veronese,* Rome, 1984.

PALLUCHINI, P.: *Tiziano,* 2 vols., Florence, 1969.

PALLUCHINI, P. - ROSSI, P.: *Tintoretto. Le opere sacre e profane,* 1990.

PIGNATTI, T.: *Veronese. L'opera completa,* Milan, 1976.

ROSAND, D.: *Painting In Cinquecento Venice: Titian, Veronese, Tintoretto,* New Haven-London, 1982.

WETHEY, H. E.: *The Paintings of Titian. Complete edition,* 3 vols., London, 1969, 1971, 1975.

General Information on the Prado Museum

EDIFICIO VILLANUEVA
Paseo del Prado, s/n
28014 Madrid
Telephone:
(91) 330-2800
Fax:
(91) 330-2856
Information:
(91) 330-2900
Wheelchair access available

VISITING HOURS
Tuesday through Saturday:
9:00 a.m. to 7:00 p.m.
Sundays and holidays:
9:00 a.m. to 2:00 p.m.
Closed on *Mondays*

ENTRANCE FEES
General Admission   *500 ptas*

Spanish youth card, student
card, or international equiva-
lents.
Cultural and education group
rates (by advance request)
(91) 330-2825)   *250 ptas*

Senior citizens over 65 or
pensioners.
Members of the Fundación
Amigos del Museo del Prado.
Cultural and educational vol-
unteers   *Free*

Free General Admission
Days
Saturdays, from 2:30 p.m. to
7:00 p.m.
Sundays, from 9:00 a.m. to
2:00 p.m.

Coffee Shop
Tuesday to Saturday:
9:30 a.m. to 6:30 p.m
Sundays and holidays:
9:30 a.m. to 1:30 p.m.

Restaurant
Monday to Saturday:
9:30 a.m. to 6:30 p.m.

Shops
Tuesday to Saturday:
9:30 a.m. to 6:30 p.m.
Sundays and holidays:
9:30 a.m. to 1:30 p.m.

HOW TO GET THERE
Metro:
Atocha, Banco and Retiro
stations

Bus:
Numbers 9, 10, 14, 19, 27,
34, 37, 45

From the airport:
Airport shuttle bus to Plaza d
Colón, then Nº. 27 bus

General Information about the
Fundación Amigos del Museo
del Prado

Museo del Prado
Claudio Coello, 73, 6ª
28001 Madrid
Tel.: (91) 431-3990
Fax: (91) 431-5155

Office hours:
Monday to Friday, from 9:30 a.m
to 2:30 p.m.